THE RUBAIYAT OF OMAR KHAYYAM

TRANSLATED BY EDWARD FITZGERALD

Introduction by John Baldock

ARCTURUS

ARCTURUS

This edition published in 2010 by Arcturus Publishing Limited
26/27 Bickels Yard, 151–153 Bermondsey Street,
London SE1 3HA

ISBN: 978-1-84837-487-4
AD001351EN

Printed in China

CONTENTS

INTRODUCTION

No other poem has ever seized the public imagination in quite the same way as *The Rubáiyát of Omar Khayyám* and yet few copies, if any, were sold when Edward Fitzgerald published it anonymously in 1859. Two years later what was left of the original print run of 250 copies was placed, priced at one penny a copy, in a remainder box outside a London bookshop. The book might well have sunk without trace but for its chance discovery by some friends of Dante Gabriel Rossetti, the poet, painter and co-founder of the Pre-Raphaelite Brotherhood, who gave it to the artist as a gift. Rossetti shared his enthusiasm for the book with his fellow Pre-Raphaelites and friends, including the poet Swinburne and William Morris, the designer, illustrator and author. Within a few years the *Rubáiyát* had achieved an unprecedented popularity on both sides of the Atlantic thanks to an article by Charles Eliot Norton in the influential *North American Review*. By 2009, the 150th anniversary of its first publication, more than 1,350 versions of the *Rubáiyát* were said to have been published in the West and it had been translated into 70 languages.

What was it about this translation of the work of an 11th-century Persian poet that saw it emerge from a remainder box outside a bookshop to become an international phenomenon? First, there was the mid 19th-century's fascination for the Orient that was already in evidence much earlier in the century — for example, Coleridge's *Kubla Khan* (1816), Shelley's *Ozymandias* (1818), Edgar Allan Poe's *Tamerlane* (1827) and *Al Aaraaf* (1829); the fashion for neo-Moorish architecture in both Europe and the USA; and the Orientalist works of painters such as John Frederick Lewis in England and Delacroix and Ingres in France. The young William Morris had been beguiled by the oriental stories in the *Arabian Nights* and in the 1870s, after Rossetti had introduced him to the *Rubáiyát,* he produced an illuminated manuscript edition of it with illustrations by Edward Burne-Jones, the Pre-Raphaelite painter.

Secondly, the evident appeal of the exotic verbal imagery of the *Rubáiyát* for the book illustrators of the second half of the 19th century coincided with advances in wood-engraved colour illustration and, towards the end of the century, the introduction of photographic and colour half-tone printing processes. One particular edition of the *Rubáiyát* to benefit from these new techniques was illustrated by Edmund Dulac, some of whose illustrations are reproduced here.

Another contributory factor to the popular success of the *Rubáiyát* in the late 19th and early 20th centuries was the appeal of its sensual, hedonistic tone for those who were tiring of the moral values imposed by Victorian society. Moreover, the poem's references to the transience of human existence resonated with both the Victorian preoccupation with death and the *fin-de-siècle* atmosphere that prevailed as the 19th century drew to a close. In North America, the popularity of the poem was fuelled by clever marketing and a constant flow of related products — the term 'Omariana' was coined to describe the latter. It became so widely popular in the USA that it inspired numerous parodies including *The Rubaiyat of a Persian Kitten* by Oliver Herford and *The Rubaiyat of Omar Khayyam, Jr.*, by the humourist Wallace Irwin. The poem's frequent references to the pleasures of drinking wine inspired J L Duff's punningly titled parody *The Rubaiyat of Ohow Dryyam*, an 'elegy for the death of alcohol due to Prohibition', but also led the Temperance movement to label the *Rubáiyát* 'a Bible for drunkards'.

Although the *Rubáiyát* may no longer bask in the fame it enjoyed in the late 19th and first half of the 20th century, its continuing popularity is undeniable, as evidenced in the numerous exhibitions that were organized in 2009 to celebrate the 150th anniversary of its first publication in the West, and the 200th anniversary of the birth of Khayyam's translator, Edward Fitzgerald.

Born into a wealthy Suffolk family in 1809, Fitzgerald was educated at King Edward VI Grammar School in Bury St Edmunds. In 1826 he went to Trinity College, Cambridge, where among those with whom he formed lasting friendships was the poet William Makepeace Thackeray. After Cambridge he returned to the family home and was to spend most of the rest of his life in the county of Suffolk, apart from a few months in Paris between 1830 and 1831 and visits to his friends in London, Oxford and elsewhere. It was while living at Woodbridge that Fitzgerald met and befriended the Quaker poet, Bernard Barton. After Barton's death in 1849, his daughter Lucy published a selection of his poems and letters for which Fitzgerald wrote the introduction. In late 1852 his friend Edward Byles Cowell, who was studying Persian at Oxford University, encouraged Fitzgerald to study Persian too. Cowell was also to play a further, more significant part in the genesis of the *Rubáiyát*.

Although Cowell was 17 years younger than Fitzgerald, the two had formed a close friendship following their initial meeting in 1844. Cowell married in 1845 and began his Persian studies at Oxford University in 1849. However, his real interest was Sanskrit and when he graduated in 1854 he expressed the intention of going to India to further both his studies and his career, much to Fitzgerald's chagrin.

While cataloguing Persian manuscripts in the Bodleian Library in April 1856, Cowell came across a 15th-century compilation of Omar Khayyam's poetry that he transcribed, giving a copy to Fitzgerald when the latter came to stay with him in July. The brevity of Fitzgerald's 'thank-you' letter suggests that he was already deeply affected by the imminent departure of his friend and Persian tutor, who had by then secured a post in Calcutta.

In November 1856, two months after the Cowells had left for India, Fitzgerald married Lucy Barton. Meanwhile, Cowell had discovered in Calcutta another manuscript of Khayyam's poetry, somewhat longer than the one he had found in Oxford, of which he had a copy made and sent to Fitzgerald. After Cowell's departure for India, Fitzgerald had continued with the work of translating the first collection of Khayyam's poetry and the arrival of this second manuscript in June 1857, by which time his marriage was all but over, seems to have spurred him on to complete the translation.

The ill-fated first edition of the *Rubáiyát* was published in February or March 1859. Fitzgerald paid for the printing himself and published the work anonymously with the help of Bernard Quaritch, whose name was printed in the book as titular publisher. Fitzgerald kept 40 copies and passed the rest of the print run of 250 to Quaritch for sale and distribution from his shop in Castle Street, near Leicester Square, but it is debatable whether any copies were sold. An unknown number of copies were lost when Quaritch moved his offices to premises in Piccadilly, and whatever was left of the original print-run was placed ignominiously in the remainder box outside the Castle Street shop. Ironically, this turned out to be the salvation of the *Rubáiyát*, for it was there that it was discovered by Rossetti's friends.

The word *rubaiyat*, meaning 'collection of quatrains', is derived from the *rubai* or four-line stanza which became a popular poetic form in Persia during the 11th century, offering a pithy alternative to the established tradition of long and obsequious courtly poems. In contrast to the latter, the *rubai* is essentially a free-standing entity in which the endings of the first, second and fourth lines rhyme, but the ending of the third line need not necessarily rhyme with the other three. While Fitzgerald respected the rhyming of Khayyam's quatrains, he broke with convention by arranging the individual stanzas so that they became linked together in a continuous poem which follows the poet's train of thought over the course of a single day as it progresses from dawn to nightfall. Fitzgerald also exercised considerable poetic licence in that he sometimes dovetailed together lines from different quatrains and is even said to have composed some of the quatrains himself. The first edition of the *Rubáiyát* comprised 75 stanzas. After its publication, Fitzgerald continued work on his translation of Khayyam's quatrains and in 1868 published a second edition in which the poem was extended to 110 stanzas. Third and fourth editions appeared in 1872 and 1879 respectively, each with 101 stanzas. However, Fitzgerald's literary activities were not confined to the *Rubáiyát*. He translated a number of plays by Calderón and reworked the classic Greek tragedies of Agamemnon and Oedipus. He also contributed to columns in local journals and his friendship with George Crabbe, grandson of the Suffolk-born poet and clergyman George Crabbe (1754–1832), led to the production of *Readings in Crabbe* — a selection of Crabbe the elder's writings — which was published privately in 1879.

Four years later, on 14 June 1883, Fitzgerald died while staying with Crabbe at the Old Rectory in Merton, Norfolk. His body was returned to Suffolk and buried in a grave next to the family mausoleum in the churchyard at Boulge, near Woodbridge, and it is said that a rose bush at the head of the grave comes from a cutting taken from Omar Khayyam's grave in Iran. A fifth edition of the *Rubáiyát* based on Fitzgerald's own manuscript revisions to the fourth edition was published posthumously in 1889. It is the text of this fifth edition that is presented in the following pages.

OMAR KHAYYAM (1044/48–1123/31)

Omar Khayyam was born in Nishapur, in the Persian province of Khorasan. At the time of Khayyam's birth, Nishapur was one of the largest cities in the world and the most important centre of culture and learning within the Islamic empire, surpassing Baghdad and Cairo. Although Khayyam is best known in the West as a poet, in his native Persia he was both a renowned astronomer — the Jalali calendar, which was in use in Persia until the 20th century, is said to have been based on his accurate calculation of the length of one year — and a respected mathematician whose treatises on algebra and geometry have made a major contribution to these fields. A number of philosophical works have also been attributed to him and it is widely held that he was a follower of the influential philosopher Ibn Sina (known as Avicenna in the West).

As far as his poetic writings are concerned, the number of quatrains attributed to Khayyam varies from about 1,000 to over 2,000. However, some scholars maintain that not all the quatrains attributed to him are authentic — it was customary in many ancient and medieval cultures for lesser-known authors to sign their writings with the name of a more famous figure in order for their work to receive greater recognition than it would if published under their own name. Another possible explanation for the uncertainty about the number of quatrains written by Khayyam is that the city of Nishapur suffered the same fate as other great centres of learning in Khorasan during the Mongol invasion of the 1220s — it was razed to the ground, its universities and libraries destroyed and its inhabitants massacred.

There is some debate as to whether Khayyam was a Sufi (an Islamic mystic). Whether he was or not, we cannot be sure; what is certain is that the verbal imagery of the *Rubáiyát* owes much to the Persian Sufi poets, in particular Abu Sa'id (978–1061) who had popularized the use of poetry, especially the newly-invented *rubai*, as a medium for expressing the mystical ideas and spiritual states associated with Sufism. The essence of Sufi teaching is the attainment of a unified state of consciousness in which our personal consciousness merges with what can best be described as a state of 'universal consciousness'. Sufis characterize this transformed state of consciousness as the union of the lover with the Beloved, or as union with God, which is why much Sufi poetry employs the language of love or alludes to the great love stories of the past alongside allusions to the Qur'an. Similarly, poetic references to drinking or getting drunk on wine — of which there are many in the *Rubáiyát* — are metaphors for the ecstatic states that can be experienced in this expanded state of consciousness. The *Rubáiyát* also employs the more traditional imagery of Persian poetry in its references to events and characters from Persia's pre-Islamic past — the latter had been collated in the *Shahnameh* (Book of Kings), an epic poem written around AD1000 that relates the mythical and historical past of Persia up to the Islamic conquest in the 7th century.

John Baldock

THE RUBAIYAT OF OMAR KHAYYAM

1

Wake! For the Sun, who scatter'd into flight

The Stars before him from the Field of Night,

Drives Night along with them from Heav'n,

and strikes

The Sultán's Turret with a Shaft of Light.

11

Before the phantom of False morning died,

Methought a Voice within the Tavern cried,

'When all the Temple is prepared within,

Why nods the drowsy Worshipper outside?'

III

And, as the Cock crew, those who stood before

The Tavern shouted — 'Open then the Door!

You know how little while we have to stay,

And, once departed, may return no more.'

IV

Now the New Year reviving old Desires,

The thoughtful Soul to Solitude retires,

Where the WHITE HAND OF MOSES on the Bough

Puts out, and Jesus from the Ground suspires.

V

Iram indeed is gone with all his Rose,

And Jamshýd's Sev'n-ring'd Cup where

no one knows;

But still a Ruby kindles in the Vine,

And many a Garden by the Water blows.

VI

And David's lips are lockt; but in divine

High-piping Pehleví, with 'Wine! Wine! Wine!

Red Wine!' — the Nightingale cries to the Rose

That sallow cheek of hers t' incarnadine.

VII

Come, fill the Cup, and in the fire of Spring

Your Winter-garment of Repentance fling:

The Bird of Time has but a little way

To flutter — and the Bird is on the Wing.

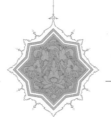

VIII

Whether at Naishápúr or Babylon,

Whether the Cup with sweet or bitter run,

The Wine of Life keeps oozing drop by drop,

The Leaves of Life keep falling one by one.

IX

Each Morn a thousand Roses brings, you say;

Yes, but where leaves the Rose of Yesterday?

And this first Summer month that brings the Rose

Shall take Jamshýd and Kaikobád away.

X

Well, let it take them! What have we to do

With Kaikobád the Great, or Kaikhosrú?

Let Zál and Rustum bluster as they will,

Or Hátim call to Supper — heed not you.

XI

With me along the strip of Herbage strown

That just divides the desert from the sown,

Where name of Slave and Sultán is forgot —

And Peace to Mahmúd on his golden Throne!

XII

A Book of Verses underneath the Bough,

A Jug of Wine, a Loaf of Bread — and Thou

Beside me singing in the Wilderness —

Oh, Wilderness were Paradise enow!

XIII

Some for the Glories of This World; and some

Sigh for the Prophet's Paradise to come;

Ah, take the Cash, and let the Credit go,

Nor heed the rumble of a distant Drum!

XIV

Look to the blowing Rose about us — 'Lo,

Laughing,' she says, 'into the world I blow,

At once the silken tassel of my Purse

Tear, and its Treasure on the Garden throw.'

XV

And those who husbanded the Golden grain,

And those who flung it to the winds like Rain,

Alike to no such aureate Earth are turn'd

As, buried once, Men want dug up again.

XVI

The Worldly Hope men set their Hearts upon

Turns Ashes — or it prospers; and anon,

Like Snow upon the Desert's dusty Face,

Lighting a little hour or two — is gone.

XVII

Think, in this batter'd Caravanserai

Whose Portals are alternate Night and Day,

How Sultán after Sultán with his Pomp

Abode his destined Hour, and went his way.

XVIII

They say the Lion and the Lizard keep

The courts where Jamshýd gloried and drank deep:

And Bahrám, that great Hunter — the Wild Ass

Stamps o'er his Head, but cannot break his Sleep.

XIX

I sometimes think that never blows so red

The Rose as where some buried Cæsar bled;

That every Hyacinth the Garden wears

Dropt in her Lap from some once lovely Head.

XX

And this reviving Herb whose tender Green

Fledges the River-Lip on which we lean —

Ah, lean upon it lightly! for who knows

From what once lovely Lip it springs unseen!

XXI

Ah, my Belovéd, fill the Cup that clears

To-day of Past Regrets and Future Fears:

To-morrow! — Why, To-morrow I may be

Myself with Yesterday's Sev'n Thousand Years.

XXII

For some we loved, the loveliest and the best

That from his Vintage rolling Time hath prest,

Have drunk their Cup a Round or two before,

And one by one crept silently to rest.

XXIII

And we, that now make merry in the Room

They left, and Summer dresses in new bloom,

Ourselves must we beneath the Couch of Earth

Descend — ourselves to make a Couch — for whom?

XXIV

Ah, make the most of what we yet may spend,

Before we too into the Dust descend;

Dust into Dust, and under Dust to lie,

Sans Wine, sans Song, sans Singer, and — sans End!

XXV

Alike for those who for To-day prepare,

And those that after some To-morrow stare,

A Muezzín from the Tower of Darkness cries

'Fools! your Reward is neither Here nor There.'

XXVI

Why, all the Saints and Sages who discuss'd

Of the Two Worlds so wisely — they are thrust

Like foolish Prophets forth; their Words to Scorn

Are scatter'd, and their Mouths are stopt with Dust.

XXVII

Myself when young did eagerly frequent

Doctor and Saint, and heard great argument

About it and about: but evermore

Came out by the same door where in I went.

XXVIII

With them the seed of Wisdom did I sow,

And with mine own hand wrought to make it grow;

And this was all the Harvest that I reap'd —

'I came like Water, and like Wind I go.'

XXIX

Into this Universe, and *Why* not knowing

Nor *Whence*, like Water willy-nilly flowing;

And out of it, as Wind along the Waste,

I know not *Whither*, willy-nilly blowing.

XXX

What, without asking, hither hurried *Whence*?

And, without asking, *Whither* hurried hence!

Oh, many a Cup of this forbidden Wine

Must drown the memory of that insolence!

XXXI

Up from Earth's Centre through the Seventh Gate

I rose, and on the Throne of Saturn sate;

And many a Knot unravel'd by the Road;

But not the Master-knot of Human Fate.

XXXII

There was the Door to which I found no Key;

There was the Veil through which I might not see:

Some little talk awhile of ME and THEE

There was — and then no more of THEE and ME.

XXXIII

Earth could not answer; nor the Seas that mourn

In flowing Purple, of their Lord Forlorn;

Nor rolling Heaven, with all his Signs reveal'd

And hidden by the sleeve of Night and Morn.

XXXIV

Then of the THEE in ME who works behind

The Veil, I lifted up my hands to find

A lamp amid the Darkness; and I heard,

As from Without — 'THE ME WITHIN THEE BLIND!'

XXXV

Then to the lip of this poor earthen Urn

I lean'd, the Secret of my Life to learn:

And Lip to Lip it murmur'd — 'While you live

Drink! — for, once dead, you never shall return.'

XXXVI

I think the Vessel, that with fugitive

Articulation answer'd, once did live,

And drink; and Ah! the passive Lip I kiss'd,

How many Kisses might it take — and give!

XXXVII

For I remember stopping by the way

To watch a Potter thumping his wet Clay:

And with its all-obliterated Tongue

It murmur'd — 'Gently, Brother, gently, pray!'

XXXVIII

And has not such a Story from of Old

Down Man's successive generations roll'd

Of such a clod of saturated Earth

Cast by the Maker into Human mould?

XXXIX

And not a drop that from our Cups we throw

For Earth to drink of, but may steal below

To quench the fire of Anguish in some Eye

There hidden — far beneath, and long ago.

XL

As then the Tulip for her morning sup

Of Heav'nly Vintage from the soil looks up,

Do you devoutly do the like, till Heav'n

To Earth invert you — like an empty Cup.

XLI

Perplext no more with Human or Divine,

To-morrow's tangle to the winds resign,

And lose your fingers in the tresses of

The Cypress-slender Minister of Wine.

XLII

And if the Wine you drink, the Lip you press

End in what All begins and ends in — Yes;

Think then you are To-day what Yester-day

You were — To-morrow you shall not be less.

XLIII

So when that Angel of the darker Drink

At last shall find you by the river-brink,

And, offering his Cup, invite your Soul

Forth to your Lips to quaff — you shall not shrink.

XLIV

Why, if the Soul can fling the Dust aside,

And naked on the Air of Heaven ride,

Were't not a Shame — were't not a Shame for him

In this clay carcase crippled to abide?

XLV

'Tis but a Tent where takes his one day's rest

A Sultán to the realm of Death addrest;

The Sultán rises, and the dark Ferrásh

Strikes, and prepares it for another Guest.

XLVI

And fear not lest Existence closing your

Account, and mine, should know the like no more;

The Eternal Sákí from that Bowl has pour'd

Millions of Bubbles like us, and will pour.

XLVII

When You and I behind the Veil are past,

Oh, but the long, long while the World shall last,

Which of our Coming and Departure heeds

As the Sea's self should heed a pebble-cast.

XLVIII

A Moment's Halt — a momentary taste

Of Being from the Well amid the Waste —

And Lo! — the phantom Caravan has reach'd

The Nothing it set out from — Oh, make haste!

XLIX

Would you that spangle of Existence spend

About THE SECRET — quick about it, Friend!

A Hair perhaps divides the False and True —

And upon what, prithee, may life depend?

L

A Hair perhaps divides the False and True;

Yes; and a single Alif were the clue —

Could you but find it — to the Treasure-house,

And peradventure to THE MASTER too;

LI

Whose secret Presence, through Creation's veins

Running Quicksilver-like eludes your pains;

Taking all shapes from Máh to Máhi; and

They change and perish all — but He remains;

LII

A moment guess'd — then back behind the Fold

Immerst of Darkness round the Drama roll'd

Which, for the Pastime of Eternity,

He doth Himself contrive, enact, behold.

LIII

But if in vain, down on the stubborn floor

Of Earth, and up to Heav'n's unopening Door,

You gaze TO-DAY, while You are You — how then

TO-MORROW, when You shall be You no more?

LIV

Waste not your Hour, nor in the vain pursuit

Of This and That endeavour and dispute;

Better be jocund with the fruitful Grape

Than sadden after none, or bitter, Fruit.

LV

You know, my Friends, with what a brave Carouse

I made a Second Marriage in my house;

Divorced old barren Reason from my Bed,

And took the Daughter of the Vine to Spouse.

LVI

For 'Is' and 'Is-not' though with Rule and Line

And 'Up-and-down' by Logic I define,

Of all that one should care to fathom, I

Was never deep in anything but — Wine.

LVII

Ah, but my Computations, People say,

Reduced the Year to better reckoning? — Nay

'Twas only striking from the Calendar

Unborn To-morrow, and dead Yesterday.

LVIII

And lately, by the Tavern Door agape,

Came shining through the Dusk an Angel Shape

Bearing a Vessel on his Shoulder; and

He bid me taste of it; and 'twas — the Grape!

LIX

The Grape that can with Logic absolute

The Two-and-Seventy jarring Sects confute:

The sovereign Alchemist that in a trice

Life's leaden metal into Gold transmute:

LX

The mighty Mahmúd, Allah-breathing Lord,

That all the misbelieving and black Horde

Of Fears and Sorrows that infest the Soul

Scatters before him with his whirlwind Sword.

LXI

Why, be this Juice the growth of God, who dare

Blaspheme the twisted tendril as a Snare?

A Blessing, we should use it, should we not?

And if a Curse — why, then, Who set it there?

LXII

I must abjure the Balm of Life, I must,

Scared by some After-reckoning ta'en on trust,

Or lured with Hope of some Diviner Drink,

To fill the Cup — when crumbled into Dust!

LXIII

Oh threats of Hell and Hopes of Paradise!

One thing at least is certain — *This* Life flies;

One thing is certain and the rest is Lies;

The Flower that once has blown for ever dies.

LXIV

Strange, is it not? that of the myriads who

Before us pass'd the door of Darkness through,

Not one returns to tell us of the Road,

Which to discover we must travel too.

LXV

The Revelations of Devout and Learn'd

Who rose before us, and as Prophets burn'd,

Are all but Stories, which, awoke from Sleep,

They told their comrades, and to Sleep return'd.

LXVI

I sent my Soul through the Invisible,

Some letter of that After-life to spell:

And by and by my Soul return'd to me,

And answer'd 'I Myself am Heav'n and Hell:'

LXVII

Heav'n but the Vision of fulfill'd Desire,

And Hell the Shadow from a Soul on fire,

Cast on the Darkness into which Ourselves,

So late emerged from, shall so soon expire.

LXVIII

We are no other than a moving row

Of Magic Shadow-shapes that come and go

Round with the Sun-illumined Lantern held

In Midnight by the Master of the Show;

LXIX

But helpless Pieces of the Game He plays

Upon this Chequer-board of Nights and Days;

Hither and thither moves, and checks, and slays,

And one by one back in the Closet lays.

LXX

The Ball no question makes of Ayes and Noes,

But Here or There as strikes the Player goes;

And He that toss'd you down into the Field,

He knows about it all — HE knows — HE knows!

LXXI

The Moving Finger writes; and, having writ,

Moves on: nor all your Piety nor Wit

Shall lure it back to cancel half a Line,

Nor all your Tears wash out a Word of it.

LXXII

And that inverted Bowl they call the Sky,

Whereunder crawling coop'd we live and die,

Lift not your hands to *It* for help — for It

As impotently moves as you or I.

LXXIII

With Earth's first Clay They did the Last Man knead,

And there of the Last Harvest sow'd the Seed:

And the first Morning of Creation wrote

What the Last Dawn of Reckoning shall read.

LXXIV

YESTERDAY *This* Day's Madness did prepare;

TO-MORROW's Silence, Triumph, or Despair:

Drink! for you know not whence you came,

nor why:

Drink! for you know not why you go, nor where.

LXXV

I tell you this — When, started from the Goal,

Over the flaming shoulders of the Foal

Of Heav'n Parwín and Mushtarí they flung

In my predestined Plot of Dust and Soul.

LXXVI

The Vine had struck a fibre: which about

If clings my Being — let the Dervish flout;

Of my Base metal may be filed a Key,

That shall unlock the Door he howls without.

LXXVII

And this I know: whether the one True Light

Kindle to Love, or Wrath consume me quite,

One Flash of It within the Tavern caught

Better than in the Temple lost outright.

LXXVIII

What! out of senseless Nothing to provoke

A conscious Something to resent the yoke

Of unpermitted Pleasure, under pain

Of Everlasting Penalties, if broke!

LXXIX

What! from his helpless Creature be repaid

Pure Gold for what he lent him dross-allay'd —

Sue for a Debt he never did contract,

And cannot answer — Oh, the sorry trade!

LXXX

Oh, Thou, who didst with pitfall and with gin

Beset the Road I was to wander in,

Thou wilt not with Predestined Evil round

Enmesh, and then impute my Fall to Sin!

LXXXI

Oh, Thou, who Man of baser Earth didst make,

And ev'n with Paradise devise the Snake:

For all the Sin wherewith the Face of Man

Is blacken'd — Man's forgiveness give — and take!

*****

LXXXII

As under cover of departing Day

Slunk hunger-stricken Ramazán away,

Once more within the Potter's house alone

I stood, surrounded by the Shapes of Clay.

LXXXIII

Shapes of all Sorts and Sizes, great and small,

That stood along the floor and by the wall;

And some loquacious Vessels were; and some

Listen'd perhaps, but never talk'd at all.

LXXXIV

Said one among them — 'Surely not in vain

My substance of the common Earth was ta'en

And to this Figure moulded, to be broke,

Or trampled back to shapeless Earth again.'

LXXXV

Then said a Second — 'Ne'er a peevish Boy

Would break the Bowl from which he drank in joy;

And He that with his hand the Vessel made

Will surely not in after Wrath destroy.'

LXXXVI

After a momentary silence spake

Some Vessel of a more ungainly Make;

'They sneer at me for leaning all awry:

What! did the Hand then of the Potter shake?'

LXXXVII

Whereat some one of the loquacious Lot —

I think a Súfi pipkin — waxing hot —

'All this of Pot and Potter — Tell me then,

Who is the Potter, pray, and who the Pot?'

LXXXVIII

'Why,' said another, 'Some there are who tell

Of one who threatens he will toss to Hell

The luckless Pots he marr'd in making — Pish!

He's a Good Fellow, and 'twill all be well.'

LXXXIX

'Well,' murmur'd one, 'Let whoso make or buy,

My Clay with long Oblivion is gone dry:

But fill me with the old familiar Juice,

Methinks I might recover by and by.'

XC

So while the Vessels one by one were speaking,

The little Moon look'd in that all were seeking:

And then they jogg'd each other, 'Brother! Brother!

Now for the Porter's shoulder-knot a-creaking!'

*****

XCI

Ah, with the Grape my fading life provide,

And wash the Body whence the Life has died,

And lay me, shrouded in the living Leaf,

By some not unfrequented Garden-side.

XCII

That ev'n my buried Ashes such a snare

Of Vintage shall fling up into the Air

As not a True-believer passing by

But shall be overtaken unaware.

XCIII

Indeed the Idols I have loved so long

Have done my credit in this World much wrong:

Have drown'd my Glory in a shallow Cup

And sold my Reputation for a Song.

XCIV

Indeed, indeed, Repentance oft before

I swore — but was I sober when I swore?

And then and then came Spring, and Rose-in-hand

My thread-bare Penitence apieces tore.

XCV

And much as Wine has play'd the Infidel,

And robb'd me of my Robe of Honour — Well,

I wonder often what the Vintners buy

One half so precious as the stuff they sell.

XCVI

Yet Ah, that Spring should vanish with the Rose!

That Youth's sweet-scented manuscript

should close!

The Nightingale that in the branches sang,

Ah, whence, and whither flown again, who knows!

XCVII

Would but the Desert of the Fountain yield

One glimpse — if dimly, yet indeed, reveal'd,

To which the fainting Traveller might spring,

As springs the trampled herbage of the field!

XCVIII

Would but some wingéd Angel ere too late

Arrest the yet unfolded Roll of Fate,

And make the stern Recorder otherwise

Enregister, or quite obliterate!

XCIX

Ah, Love! could you and I with Him conspire

To grasp this sorry Scheme of Things entire,

Would not we shatter it to bits — and then

Re-mould it nearer to the Heart's Desire!

*****

☾

Yon rising Moon that looks for us again —

How oft hereafter will she wax and wane;

How oft hereafter rising look for us

Through this same Garden — and for *one* in vain!

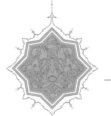

CI

And when like her, oh, Sákí, you shall pass

Among the Guests Star-scatter'd on the Grass,

And in your joyous errand reach the spot

Where I made One — turn down an empty Glass!

TAMÁM

EXPLANATORY NOTES

II

'Before the phantom of False morning died…': The false dawn or zodiacal light occurs in the east about an hour before sunrise, with the latter serving as a sign for the muezzin to call out from a minaret of the mosque, summoning Muslims to perform the first of the five daily prayers. Here the muezzin's call is perhaps parodied by the voice from within the tavern, summoning those outside to come in and drink. An alternative interpretation is possible when we consider that in Sufi poetry the 'tavern' was the symbolic name given to the Sufis' meeting-place.

IV

'Now the New Year…': The Persian New Year is at the Vernal (Spring) Equinox.
'The white hand of Moses': mentioned in the Qur'an 7:108 and Exodus 4:6, with the latter describing it 'as white as snow.' Although snow is still on the ground at this time of year, the white blossom on the boughs of the sweet almond tree announces the arrival of spring. The poet also associates the green shoots of new life with the life-giving breath of Jesus (suspire = to breathe) for the Qur'an (3:49) tells us how, as a sign of the authority God has invested in him, Jesus will make a bird from a lump of clay and breathe into it and it will become a living bird.

V

'Iram indeed is gone…': The lost city of Iram (Ubar) is mentioned in the Qur'an (89:6–7). The city was built by the people of 'Ad, the descendants of Noah, and had 'lofty pillars' (a sign of both its prosperity and its arrogance). Iram was destroyed by God because its inhabitants were idol worshippers.
'Jamshýd's Sev'n-ring'd Cup…': In Persian mythology, Shah Jamshid (Fitzgerald's 'Jamshýd') ruled the world for 300 years and is credited with introducing, among other things, the mining of jewels and precious metals, wine-making, navigation and healing. He is said to have owned a magical seven-ringed cup containing the elixir of immortal life. The cup also enabled Jamshid to watch over the entire world as well as look into the future.

EXPLANATORY NOTES

VI

'And David's lips are lockt…': King David, the psalmist (Qur'an 17:56).

'High-piping Pehlevi…': Pehlevi or Middle Persian was a language of Persia during the Sassanid dynasty (AD224–651).

The rose and nightingale (*gul-u-bulbul*) is one of the most evocative and widely used verbal images of Persian poetry. In many ancient traditions a bird was a symbol for the human soul and the nightingale is often interpreted as the soul singing to the Beloved. One tradition holds that the rose was originally white but the nightingale, filled with passionate song, embraced the rose. A thorn pierced the bird's heart and its blood coloured the rose red.

IX and X

Kaikobád (Kai Kobad): Mythical Persian king, founder of the Kayani dynasty.

Kaikhosrú (Kai Khosrow): Son of Kai Kobad.

Zal and Rustam: Father and son, both mythical Persian warriors.

Hátim (Hatim Tai): A legendary figure famous for his generosity.

XI

'Slave and Sultan': An allusion to Sultan Mahmud of Ghazna (see below) and his slave, Ayaz. The story of the chaste love affair between the two men and their mutual devotion to each other is one of the great love stories of Persian literature.

Mahmúd: Mahmud of Ghazna (AD971–1030) was the Turkic founder of the Ghaznavid Empire, which extended over much of modern Afghanistan, Iran, Pakistan and north-west India. A patron of the arts and learning, he commissioned the poet Firdausi to write the *Shahnameh* (see page 9). Mahmud was the first ruler to carry the title of Sultan (meaning 'authority').

XIII

'the Prophet's Paradise': A reference to the Islamic paradise, described by the Prophet Muhammad in the Qur'an.

'a distant Drum': The drum was used as a traditional rallying call. For Sufi poets, the falconer sounding his drum to summon the falcon back to him was associated with a verse from the Qur'an: 'We belong to Allah, and unto Him we are returning' (Qur'an 2:156).

XVII

Caravanserai: Similar to European coaching inns, caravanserai were situated along trade routes and provided a place for travellers to stay overnight and refresh themselves and their animals after a day's journey. As here, the caravanserai is often used as a metaphor for the world and the transitory nature of human existence.

XVIII

'the Lion and the lizard': After the death of the legendary Jamshid, the civilization he had reigned over for 300 years fell into decay — a state alluded to by the presence of wildlife occupying the site of his former palace.

Bahram V, Sassanid ruler of Persia (AD421–438), also known as Bahram Gur because of his passion for hunting the wild ass or onager (Persian *gur*). There is a pun here on the word *gur*, which also means 'grave'. Bahram is said to have died when his horse sank into a swamp, a habitat favoured by the wild ass which is too light to sink in the mire.

XIX

In Persian poetry the flowers of the hyacinth are likened to the curled locks of the hair of the Beloved.

XXV

Muezzín: a muezzin calls the faithful to prayer from a minaret on a mosque.

XXVI and XXVII

'Saints and Sages' (XXVI), 'Doctor and Saint' (XXVII): Saints = Sufi mystics or saints; sages and doctors = philosophers and jurists (religious lawyers). Khayyam appears to mock the apparent futility of their discussions and arguments about the nature of the two worlds.

'the Two Worlds': The material and the spiritual worlds (see also XLI).

XXXI

'the Seventh Gate': Possibly an allusion to the religious tradition that saints and martyrs ascend through the heavenly realms said to lie beyond this world, and are enthroned in the seventh heaven or Paradise. Khayyam, the sceptical astronomer, substitutes Saturn (one of the seven planets) for the seventh heaven.

XXXII

'Me and Thee': the lover or human soul and the Beloved. The name Fitzgerald gave to the boat he had built for a close friend Joseph 'Posh' Fletcher was *Meum and Tuum*.

XXXV to XXXVII

Urn, vessel, potter and clay: Stories about a potter moulding a lump of clay into a pot allude to the creation of the first human beings who, according to the creation myths of many of the world's religious traditions, were moulded by the Creator from a lump of earth.

XL

The flower of the tulip is often mentioned in Persian poetry because it is shaped like a wine cup or goblet.

XLI

'Human or Divine': As in XXVI, a reference to the 'two worlds'.

XLIII

'Angel of the darker Drink': Azrael, the angel of death.

XLIV

The description of the body as a 'clay carcase [carcass]' recalls the earlier allusions to the potter and the lump of clay (see XXXVII).

XLV

''Tis but a Tent': A reflection on the transitory nature of human existence.
Ferrásh: a servant responsible for setting up tents and spreading carpets (*farsh*) and cushions. On occasion, he also acted as an executioner.

XLVI

Sákí = 'cupbearer' in Persian. The Eternal Saki is the Beloved who pours out the wine of life and love.

XLIX

'the False and True': Like the human and spiritual realms, these are often said to be separated by no more than a hair's breadth.

L

Alif, the first letter of the Persian or Farsi alphabet, is written as a simple, vertical stroke: |.

LI

The Persian word *mah* translates as fish or moon, while *Mah* is the name of the Zoroastrian deity who personifies the moon. The Persian expression *az mah ta mahi* (from moon to mah-fish) means 'everything'.

LVI

'Is and Is-Not' and 'Up-and-Down': Possible references to debates engaged in by mystics and philosophers about 'being and not-being', 'created and uncreated' and the 'higher and lower worlds'. Khayyam states that he prefers logic to abstract ideas, adding in a self-mocking vein that the only thing that ever held a deep interest for him was wine.

LVII

'Ah, but my Computations…': A reference to Khayyam's role in reforming the Persian calendar. The corrected 'Jalali calendar' was in use until the 20th century and is the basis of the modern Iranian calendar.

LIX

According to tradition, the Prophet Muhammad stated that the Islamic community would fragment into seventy-three sects. The members of only one of these sects would remain faithful to the teachings of the Prophet; the other seventy-two would end up in the fires of hell.

LXX

In Persian poetry the game of polo was employed as a metaphor for human life in which the ball (the individual human being) is whacked to and fro by the mallet of the player (God).

EXPLANATORY NOTES

LXXV
'Parwín and Mushtarí':The Pleiades and Jupiter.

LXXVI
Dervish = poor (man).A term generally used to denote an aspiring Sufi.

LXXVII
'the one True Light': Possibly an allusion to a chapter (*surah*) of the Qur'an, Surah 24 The Light (*Al-Nur*), whose often-quoted 'Light Verse' contains the words 'God is the Light of the heavens and the earth' (24:35).

LXXX
Gin: A type of trap used for catching animals.

LXXXII
Ramazán = Ramadan, the Islamic month of fasting.

LXXXVII
Súfi = Islamic mystic. Pipkin = an earthenware cooking-pot made to be heated directly over a fire rather than in an oven.

CI
Tamám = Finished, or The End.

VARIATIONS

The number of quatrains included by Fitzgerald in the *Rubáiyát* varied over the first three editions as follows: first edition (1859) 75; second edition (1868) 110; third edition (1872) 101. The fourth (1879) and posthumous fifth edition (1889) also comprised 101 quatrains.

The text of quatrains included in the first and second editions but omitted from later editions is given below, as are examples of variations Fitzgerald made to the text of some of the quatrains in different editions of the *Rubáiyát*.

1st edition
XLV

But leave the Wise to wrangle, and with me
The Quarrel of the Universe let be:
And, in some corner of the Hubbub coucht,
Make Game of that which makes as much of Thee.

2nd edition
XIV

Were it not Folly, Spider-like to spin
The Thread of present Life away to win
What? for ourselves, who know not if we shall
Breathe out the very Breath we now breathe in!

XX

The Palace that to Heav'n his pillars threw,
And Kings the forehead on his threshold drew —
I saw the solitary Ringdove there,
And 'Coo, coo, coo,' she cried; and 'Coo, coo, coo.'

XXVIII

Another Voice, when I am sleeping, cries,
'The Flower should open with the Morning skies.'
And a retreating Whisper, as I wake —
'The Flower that once has blown for ever dies.'

VARIATIONS

XLIV

Do you, within your little hour of Grace,
The waving Cypress in your Arms enlace,
   Before the Mother back into her arms
Fold, and dissolve you in a last embrace.

LXV

If but the Vine and Love-abjuring Band
Are in the Prophet's Paradise to stand,
   Alack, I doubt the Prophet's Paradise.
Were empty as the hollow of one's Hand.

LXXVII

For let Philosopher and Doctor preach
Of what they will, and what they will not — each
   Is but one Link in an eternal Chain
That none can slip, nor break, nor over-reach.

LXXXVI

Nay, but, for terror of his wrathful Face,
I swear I will not call Injustice Grace;
   Not one Good Fellow of the Tavern but
Would kick so poor a Coward from the place.

XCIX

Whither resorting from the vernal Heat
Shall Old Acquaintance Old Acquaintance greet,
   Under the Branch that leans above the Wall
To shed his Blossom over head and feet.

CVII

Better, oh better, cancel from the Scroll
Of Universe one luckless Human Soul,
   Than drop by drop enlarge the Flood that rolls
Hoarser with Anguish as the Ages roll.

VARIATIONS

Example of Fitzgerald's variations in the opening quatrain of the *Rubáiyát*:

I (1st edition)
Awake! for Morning in the Bowl of Night
Has flung the Stone that puts the Stars to Flight:
And Lo! the Hunter of the East has caught
The Sultán's Turret in a Noose of Light.

I (2nd edition)
Wake! For the Sun behind yon Eastern height
Has chased the Sessions of the Stars from Night;
And, to the field of Heav'n ascending, strikes
The Sultán's Turret with a Shaft of Light.

I (3rd and subsequent editions)
Wake! For the Sun who scatter'd into flight
The Stars before him from the Field of Night,
Drives Night along with them from Heav'n, and strikes
The Sultán's Turret with a Shaft of Light.

Example of Fitzgerald's variations in the 3rd, 4th and 5th editions:

XXXVIII (3rd edition)
Listen — a moment listen! — Of the same
Poor Earth from which that Human Whisper came
The luckless Mould in which Mankind was cast
They did compose, and call'd him by the name.

XXXVIII (4th and 5th editions)
And has not such a Story from of Old
Down Man's successive generations roll'd
Of such a clod of saturated Earth
Cast by the Maker into Human mould?